ESSENTIAL DK COMPUTERS

INTERNET

JAVASCRIPT
AN INTRODUCTION

ABOUT THIS BOOK

Javascript: An Introduction is an easy-to-follow guide to incorporating JavaScript code into your HTML document and understanding the effects of JavaScript on the web page.

THIS BOOK WILL GIVE YOU A FLAVOR OF JavaScript as a programming language and familiarize you with how it looks as code in the HTML document. You will find advice on how to build up some basic, but widely used, JavaScript code from scratch; how to use third-party software such as Macromedia's Dreamweaver to generate code for you; and how to recognize JavaScript in other web pages, enabling you to learn from what others have done. This book is intended for PC users working with Notepad and Internet Explorer version 4 or higher, but the basic principles apply to all modern web browsers and simple text editors. You are welcome to adapt any of the scripts shown here and use them on your own web pages. It should be simple enough to substitute your own text and hyperlinks within the JavaScript code shown throughout the book. Equally

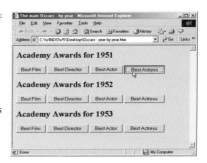

importantly, Chapter 7 of this book advises you on how to debug your scripts.

The chapters and the subsections present the information using step-by-step sequences. Virtually every step is accompanied by an illustration showing how your screen should look at each stage.

The book contains several features to help you understand both what is happening and what you need to do.

Command keys are shown in these rectangles: [Enter ←] and [Ctrl], to prevent confusion over what should be typed. Cross-references are shown in the text as left- or right-hand page icons: ⌐ and ⌐. The page number and the reference are shown at the foot of the page.

There are also boxes that explain a feature in detail, and tip boxes that provide alternative methods. Finally, at the back, you will find a glossary of common terms and a comprehensive index.

ESSENTIAL **DK** COMPUTERS

INTERNET

JAVASCRIPT
AN INTRODUCTION

BRIAN COOPER

LONDON, NEW YORK, SYDNEY, DELHI, PARIS, MUNICH, and JOHANNESBURG

Produced for Dorling Kindersley Limited by
Design Revolution Limited, Queens Park Villa,
30 West Drive, Brighton, England BN2 2GE
EDITORIAL DIRECTOR Ian Whitelaw
SENIOR DESIGNER Andy Ashdown
PROJECT EDITOR Ian Kearey
DESIGNER Paul Bowler

SENIOR EDITOR Amy Corzine
SENIOR ART EDITOR Sarah Cowley
US EDITORS Gary Werner and Margaret Parrish
DTP DESIGNER Julian Dams
PRODUCTION CONTROLLER Michelle Thomas

MANAGING EDITOR Adèle Hayward
SENIOR MANAGING ART EDITOR Nigel Duffield

First American Edition, 2001

01 02 03 04 05 10 9 8 7 6 5 4 3 2 1

First published in the United States by DK Publishing, Inc.
95 Madison Avenue, New York, New York 10016

DK Publishing offers special discounts for bulk purchases for sales promotions or
premiums. Specific, large-quantity needs can be met with special editions, including
personalized covers, excerpts of existing guides, and corporate imprints.
For more information, contact Special Markets Department, DK Publishing, Inc.,
95 Madison Avenue, New York, NY 10016 Fax: 800-600-9098.

A Cataloging in Publication record is available from the Library of Congress

ISBN 0-7894-8005-0

Color reproduced by Colourscan, Singapore
Printed and bound in Italy by Graphicom

See our complete catalog at
www.dk.com

CONTENTS

JAVASCRIPT OVERVIEW

If you are familiar with the basics of HTML, the markup
language behind web pages, you should have few problems
in understanding the basics of JavaScript.

WHAT IS JAVASCRIPT?

JavaScript is a programming language –
or, more specifically, an object-based
scripting language – but don't be put off
by the technical jargon. JavaScript is far
simpler to learn than other programming
languages, such as Java and C++.
JavaScript works with HTML to extend
your control over the web browser, and
to improve the way web pages work by
making them more dynamic and efficient.

EASIER THAN
IT LOOKS

● Since most JavaScript
effects take the form of a
few lines of text embedded
in an HTML document,
you can soon learn
sufficient programming
skills to make significant
improvements to your
website.

● Most browsers have
built-in JavaScript
compilers (the facility that
interprets and runs
JavaScript code), so users
don't need to install special
plug-ins to reap the
benefits of JavaScript code
included in a web page.

```
<SCRIPT language="JavaScript">
<!-- Hide script from older browsers
if (navigator.appCodeName == "JavaEnabled")
{
document.write("NO PROBLEM! Your Web browser is
JAVA enabled")
}

else
{
alert("PROBLEMS! Your Web browser is not JAVA
enabled. Choose the UPGRADE or NON-JAVA buttons
on the following page.")
}
//End hiding script from older brosers -->
</SCRIPT>
```

Internet
Explorer

Netscape
Communicator

Opera 4.0

Each of these web browsers contains a JavaScript compiler.

WHAT CAN JAVASCRIPT DO?

By extending the control you have over the way that the web browser works, JavaScript can produce many on-screen effects that inject added functionality to web pages to increase their attractiveness and, most importantly, their usefulness.

JAVASCRIPT CONTROLS

For instance, JavaScript can enable you to:

● Control the contents of the status bar along the foot of the window, which by default displays the relevant URL when the mouse cursor is positioned over a hyperlink.

This text has been defined in JavaScript ●

● Specify images and text to appear when the mouse pointer moves over certain areas of the screen. These areas can be images, links, or even blank areas of the page. This facility enables you to produce smooth rollover effects, swapping one image for another – for example, making a button appear to be pressed in.

● Use information from the visitor's browser to detect whether necessary software is installed, and alert the visitor or reroute them to a part of the site that is designed for their browser type.

● Use information from the visitor to personalize the page with his/her name.
● Determine the makeup of new hyperlinked windows, such as whether they are to contain toolbars, address boxes, and scroll bars.

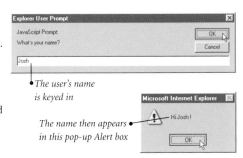

• *The user's name is keyed in*

The name then appears • in this pop-up Alert box

ADVANCED EFFECTS

JavaScript can also be used to carry out equations or create interactive games. There are many sites, such as **javascript.internet.com**, that offer complex scripts that can be pasted into your HTML documents.

OVERDOING IT

The interactivity that JavaScript offers can prove too tempting for many beginners, so use it sensibly to help the visitor, rather than just to show off. For example, if you use JavaScript to detect the visitor's browser type and version, it is irritating for the visitor just to be told that you know. It would be far better to use the information to divert the visitor to a part of the site specifically designed for users of that browser. To do this, you will need some knowledge of functions and "**if...else**" statements. These may sound complex, but they are surprisingly easy to learn ◻.

SHOWING OFF

● Using JavaScript to activate an Alert box ◻ like this one is more likely to be annoying than helpful.

JAVASCRIPT IN ACTION

You can embed JavaScript in the HTML code of any web page in your website. Before looking at an example of the code, let's look at a typical sequence of web pages that demonstrates the kind of interactivity that Javascript can produce.

1 BRINGING UP AN ALERT BOX

● The appearance and content of this Alert box on the opening screen are controlled by Javascript.

2 IDENTIFYING THE WEB BROWSER

● The ability to identify the particular web browser that the visitor is using, and to insert the browser name into the onscreen text, is a feature of JavaScript.

Learning about your browser

I see you're using the **Microsoft Internet Explorer** brow page will help you find out more about your browser. Use at the bottom of the page to visit the main browser produce or to read a history of Web browsers.

To do your own research, follow these to our lists of leading Web directories recommended search engines.

3 VIEWING TEXT IN THE STATUS BAR

● In this case, the text that appears in the status bar at the bottom of the screen, in response to the pointer passing over the link on the page, is defined in the JavaScript code.

THE JAVASCRIPT BEHIND THE EVENTS

Taking the sequence that we have just seen and looking at the HTML source code, we can see how the effects have been achieved using just a few lines of Javascript embedded in the HTML. The annotations highlight a few points about the appearance and uses of JavaScript, which are developed in this book.

This code causes the above Alert box to pop up when the page is opened •

*The **document.write** command writes everything in quotes, plus everything within the + signs, to the web page* •

*This code (**navigator.appName**) detects the visitor's browser type and version and writes the browser type dynamically to the web page* 📄

Learning about your browser

I see you're using the **Microsoft Internet Explorer** browser. This page will help you find out more about your browser. Use the buttons at the bottom of the page to visit the main browser producers' sites, or to read a history of Web browsers.

To do your own research, follow these hyperlinks to our lists of leading <u>Web directories</u> and recommended <u>search engines</u>.

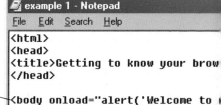

```
example 1 - Notepad
File  Edit  Search  Help
<html>
<head>
<title>Getting to know your brow
</head>

<body onload="alert('Welcome to
<h3>Learning about your browser<

<script language="JavaScript">
document.write("I see you're usi
+"</b> browser.")
</script>

This page will help you find out
buttons at the bottom of the page
producers' sites, or to read a h:
<p>
<img src="pc.jpg" align="left">
To do your own research, follow
leading <a href="http://www.inse
onMouseOver="window.status='Try
directories';return true">Web di

and recommended <a
href="http://www.insertyoursiteh
onMouseOver="window.status='Try
search engines';return true">sea
</body>
</html>
```

| 9 | JavaScript in Action | | 22 | Writing to the Document |

MAKING THINGS HAPPEN

The active elements within the windows we have just seen ⌐ (the appearance of an Alert box, the identification of the user's browser, and the text seen in the status bar when the cursor moves over the hyperlinks) are controlled by JavaScript embedded within this HTML document.

```
/title>

eb page')">
<p>

he <b>" +navigator.appName

e about your browser. Use the
 visit the main browser
ry of Web browsers.</b>

e hyperlinks to our lists of
ursitehere.com/webdir.htm"
of these recommended Web
ories</a>

com/webdir.htm"
ching with one of these top
engines</a>.
```

JAVASCRIPT SYNTAX

QUOTATION MARKS IN TEXT
Use quotation marks within text "strings" carefully, because they can seriously confuse the browser about where the code ends and the text begins. The rule is, you should use single quotations if you need to use quotation marks within double quotation marks. For example: **document.write ("Be very 'careful' about using quote marks.")**

SEMICOLONS
It is an optional, but useful, practice to end each line of code with a semicolon. This punctuation mark tells the browser unequivocally where a new line of code begins. The newer versions of the most popular web browsers may be able to work out for themselves where a new line of code begins, but now and then a missing semicolon can cause a mess.

or to read a history of Web browsers.

To do your own research, foll... to our lists of leading Web dir... recommended search engines.

🔄 Try searching with one of these top search eng

These two blocks of code specify the text that will appear in the status bar (see above) when the mouse cursor moves over the text hyperlinks ⌐

9	JavaScript in Action	34	Functions of the Status Bar

JAVASCRIPT BASICS

Recognizing where to put blocks of JavaScript code into an
HTML document is one of the first things you need to know
when approaching the language for the first time.

IDENTIFYING JAVASCRIPT

Lines of JavaScript code need to be
identified separately from HTML code. If
you look at the source code of any HTML

document containing JavaScript, the
JavaScript code is most easily recognized if
it is contained within **<script>** tags.

USING <SCRIPT> TAGS

● When code is placed
between **<script>** and
</script> tags, most
browsers assume that the
enclosed code is to be read
as JavaScript.

● Most browsers take
JavaScript to be the default,
but other scripts (VBScript,
for example) can be used
within these tags. For this
reason it is advisable to
specify the programming
language that is being used,
in this case by making the
first tag **<script language=**
"JavaScript">.

EMBED JAVASCRIPT ANYWHERE

When enclosed within
<script> tags, JavaScript
can be embedded
anywhere in an HTML
document (as long as it
doesn't conflict with
HTML rules), and as
many times as required.
If the script relates to a
button on the page, you

can place the code
adjacent to that block
of HTML on the page.
More often than not,
though, the JavaScript is
placed within the **<head>**
section of the document.
This is particularly true
where functions are
concerned ◻.

USING <HEAD> TAGS

● When you open a web page, the code between the <**head**> tags is loaded before the web page is displayed on-screen.

● In this example, an Alert box ⃞ containing the words **Welcome to our website** pops up before the web page appears on your screen.

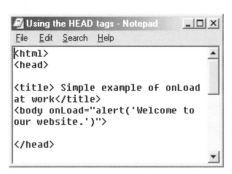

```
<html>
<head>

<title> Simple example of onLoad
at work</title>
<body onLoad="alert('Welcome to
our website.')">

</head>
```

USING A FUNCTION

● It is not obligatory for any code within <**script**> tags to appear between the <**head**> tags of the document, but it is good practice to place this code there when using a function (or functions) that you will "call" further down the page ⃞.

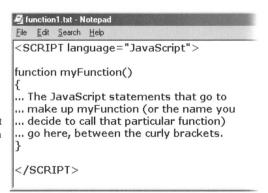

```
<SCRIPT language="JavaScript">

function myFunction()
{
... The JavaScript statements that go to
... make up myFunction (or the name you
... decide to call that particular function)
... go here, between the curly brackets.
}

</SCRIPT>
```

THE IMPORTANCE OF RECOGNIZING JAVASCRIPT

The ability to recognize JavaScript code will help you to identify those sections of code in other people's web pages that you can learn from, adapt, and use to suit your own website. Also, you sometimes need to modify the JavaScript that has been generated using third-party software. Even the best HTML design packages can sometimes get themselves into a tangle, leaving you with no other solution than to open the source code and debug the script. More often than not, this simply involves locating the problem area and removing a duplicate tag. Knowing your way around the code will also have obvious benefits when it comes to tracking down your own mistakes.

⃞ 27 **Alert Boxes**

⃞ 15 **JavaScript Functions**

JAVASCRIPT EVENT HANDLERS

Some JavaScript code does not need to be placed within <**script**> tags. Usually, these instances are known as event handlers. Examples include the commands that make events happen when the visitor clicks the mouse or moves the cursor over text or an image. Whatever appears in quotes after one of these commands is interpreted by the browser as being JavaScript and is handled accordingly.

AN EVENT HANDLER IN ACTION

● Event handlers are compound words that begin with **on**, followed by a verb beginning with a capital letter. For example: **onClick, onChange, onLoad, onSubmit,** or **onMouseOver.**

● In this example, **onUnload** is being used to call up an Alert box.

```html
<html>
<title> Simple example of onUnload at
work</title>

<body onUnload="alert('Thanks for visiting. Call
again soon!')">
This simple Web page demonstrates the onUnload
event handler at work.

<p>When you leave this Web page, or quit the Web
browser, an alert box will appear containing the
words you have specified for the alert box.

<p>Note that you do not need to use "javascript"
 tags in this example.
</body>
</html>
```

● This is the page that contains source code for the JavaScript event handler. Event handlers do not require "JavaScript" tags.

This simple Web page demonstrates the onUnload event handler at work.

When you leave this Web page, or quit the Web browser, an alert box will appear containing the words you have specified for the alert box.

Note that you do not need to use "javascript" tags in this example.

🔲 Done   🖳   🖳 My Computer

● When the user leaves the page or quits the browser, the Alert box appears.

Microsoft Internet Explorer

⚠ Thanks for visiting. Call again soon!

OK

JAVASCRIPT FUNCTIONS

JavaScript uses a programming tool called a "function" to work more efficiently. Once you understand how functions fit into the general plan, you should be able to break down a page of code into something that makes sense structurally.

THE PURPOSE OF FUNCTIONS

● A function is a named series of commands and is usually contained within the <**head**> tags.

● Once a function has been created, you can "call" it as many times as you like further down the page by using a single line of code rather than typing a long block of code into the body of the HTML.

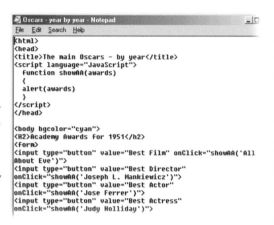

● What a function does, and what it is named, is determined by the author.

● In this case, the function **showAA** is being used to bring up an appropriate Alert box when a button is clicked.

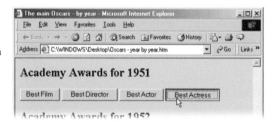

● Clicking on the **Best Actress** button causes the function to operate and bring up an Alert box containing the words **Judy Holliday**.

WRITING JAVASCRIPT IN NOTEPAD

You don't need any special software to write JavaScript. In fact, when you are starting out, it is best to use the simplest text editor at your disposal. Notepad, which is supplied with Windows 98, provides a good, no-frills tool. Whatever editor you use, you need to save your scripts in "text only" format. In this way, if you copy-and-paste JavaScript code from a saved file, you can guarantee you will not be copying hidden code placed there by the word-processing program.

1 WRITING IN NOTEPAD

● Using Notepad, you can write JavaScript directly into HTML documents, or you can write the JavaScript separately, save the file, and then copy and paste the script into an HTML document later .

● Here we are writing two scripts in a new Notepad document, making sure to give each script a brief descriptive heading that will help us identify it later.

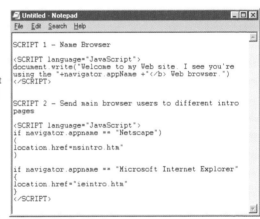

```
SCRIPT 1 - Name Browser

<SCRIPT language="JavaScript">
document.write("Welcome to my Web site. I see you're
using the "+navigator.appName +"</b> Web browser.")
</SCRIPT>

SCRIPT 2 - Send main browser users to different intro
pages

<SCRIPT language="JavaScript">
if navigator.appname == "Netscape")
(
location.href=nsintro.htm"
)

if navigator.appname == "Microsoft Internet Explorer"
{
location.href="ieintro.htm"
}
</SCRIPT>
```

2 SAVING THE DOCUMENT

● Once the scripts are complete, save the document into a suitably named folder.

● If you are creating an HTML document including JavaScript, remember to save it as an HTML document with either a **.htm** or **.html** extension.

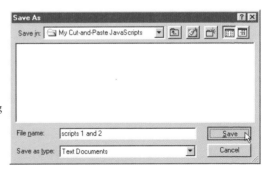

Save As		
Save in:	My Cut-and-Paste JavaScripts	
File name:	scripts 1 and 2	Save
Save as type:	Text Documents	Cancel

 17 **Copy and paste the script**

3 COPY AND PASTE THE SCRIPT

● When you are ready to embed the code in an HTML document, simply open the file in Notepad, highlight the script that you want, as shown here, and then copy it into the relevant part of the web page HTML code.

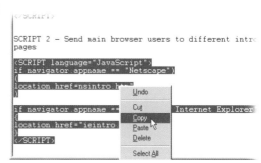

USEFUL SCRIPTING TOOLS

Nearly all the examples of JavaScript in this book have been created by keying the code in Notepad, but there is nothing to stop you from using several different web building and script editing programs to produce your JavaScript code. Remember, you can always read the JavaScript code produced in any of these programs, so you can learn from the techniques they employ and make them your own.

WYSIWYG HTML PACKAGES

● You can find many sophisticated menu-driven HTML design packages, such as Macromedia's Dreamweaver, Microsoft's FrontPage, and others, that will help simplify the process of creating JavaScript. These packages can automatically generate a wide range of JavaScript effects, such as rollover images 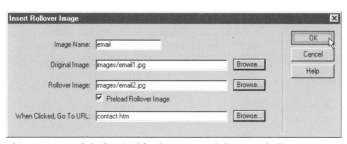.

This Dreamweaver dialog box simplifies the creation and placement of rollover images.

JAVASCRIPT EDITORS

Some excellent JavaScript editing programs, available as shareware and freeware, provide shortcuts to various common coding tasks. For example, several programs allow you to highlight a block of text and choose a menu item, and the necessary code is then generated automatically for you, saving a good deal of routine work on the keyboard.

STJS MENUMAKER

● STJS Menumaker is a good example. It is an easy-to-use freeware program that generates JavaScript drop-down menus. For more detail, see the author's site (**www. comwell.se/samuel/ software**) and follow the links.

● Here we have typed the names and URLs that will produce a drop-down menu of Mediterranean islands.

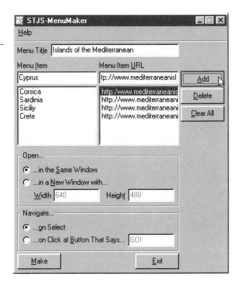

● Once you have clicked the **Make** button, a new web page is produced containing the drop-down menu you have just specified.

*The list here corresponds to the contents of the **Menu Item** box in the previous screen*

REVIEWING AND EDITING

You will regularly want to review your code as you go along. To do this, you will need to have both Notepad, containing the HTML document you are editing, and your web browser, containing the same HTML document, open at the same time.

OPENING THE SOURCE CODE

● To open the source code of a web page (this includes your HTML documents stored on your hard disk), open the file in your web browser and choose **Source** from the **View** menu.
● By default, Notepad will open, displaying the HTML document as a text file.

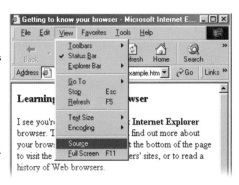

● With the web page open in the background, edit the text document. To monitor the effect of your editing on the web page, first choose **Save** from the **File** menu in Notepad.

● Now bring the web browser window to the front, click on the **Refresh** button, and review the changes.
● This is a very useful way of working because you can identify any problems as they arise, thereby saving a lot of time debugging your script later .

HIDING JAVASCRIPT

In the context of JavaScript, there are two kinds of comments that can be included in the HTML document. The first of these, discussed in a later chapter [], consists of comments keyed into the JavaScript itself that allow you to write helpful notes to yourself. The second kind consists of comments keyed into the HTML, and these serve a more important purpose when writing JavaScript. HTML comments can hide your code from old browsers that can't handle JavaScript [].

USING AN HTML COMMENT

● Older browsers that cannot display JavaScript [] may display your code as text on the page. To prevent this from happening, comments in the HTML can be used to hide JavaScript.

● The example below shows this in action. The opening of a comment in HTML is: <!--. The closing of a comment in HTML is: -->. A browser that can handle Javascript will carry out the JavaScript commands – in this example, writing text to the browser window. A browser that can't handle Javascript will simply ignore everything between the HTML comment tags.

```
html comments - Notepad
File  Edit  Search  Help
<html>
<head>
<title>HTML comments</title>
</head>

<script language="JavaScript">
<!-- Hide JavaScript from older browsers

document.write("All this text will appear in<br>");
document.write("browsers that handle JavaScript.<br>") ;
document.write("Older browsers will display <br>");
document.write("only the message in red <br>");
document.write("at the bottom of the page.<br>");

// stop hiding JavaScript -->
</script>

<hr>
<h6> <font color="red">If only this message is displayed,
you need to visit the <a href="textonly.htm">text-only
version </a> of this page.</font></h6>

</html>
```

NON-JAVASCRIPT-ENABLED BROWSERS

● Here the web page is being seen on a JavaScript-enabled browser. A link is provided to a text-only version of the page for browsers that cannot handle JavaScript. This requires more work, but will make your web page more widely available ◻.

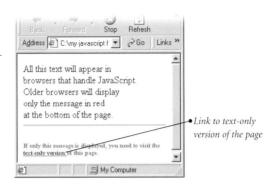

Link to text-only version of the page

CATERING FOR THE MINORITY

Catering for those visitors to your site who use non-JavaScript-enabled browsers is a site-design issue that can be tackled in a number of ways. Writing a page that contains JavaScript, but that also provides sufficient information for anyone who can't access the JavaScript material, requires careful planning. The solution depends on the nature of the web pages you are building, the information they contain, and how conscientious you are. Some authors design a separate page for users of older browsers. Others provide a link to a text-only version of the page. Some authors simply include a message that states: "Your web browser cannot cope with this page; perhaps it's time to upgrade your browser," and they leave it at that.

BROWSERS AND JAVASCRIPT

BROWSERS ABLE TO HANDLE JAVASCRIPT		BROWSERS UNABLE TO HANDLE JAVASCRIPT	
Browser	Version	Browser	Version
Netscape Navigator 2	JavaScript 1.0	AOL Browser	1.3
Netscape Navigator 3	JavaScript 1.1	Mosaic	1.3
Netscape Navigator 4+	JavaScript 1.2	Netscape Navigator	1.1
Internet Explorer 3	Jscript	Internet Explorer	1.2
Internet Explorer 4+	Jscript 1.2	Lynx	
Internet Explorer 5			
Opera 3.5, 4 and other recent browsers			

USING JAVASCRIPT

The use of JavaScript in web page source code can be extensive, but in this chapter we will look at some of the most commonly-adopted ways of using the code.

WRITING TO THE DOCUMENT

Of all the commands available in JavaScript one of the most widely used is **document.write**. This enables you to use JavaScript to write text into the browser window. The question that naturally arises, though, is why you would want to use a JavaScript command when you can do the same thing with HTML.

DYNAMIC AND STATIC WRITING

The point of the "write" command (or "method," to use the correct terminology) is that it allows you much wider options than HTML for writing information to the browser window. With HTML, the browser window only displays the text that you have written in the source code of the document. Using the **document.write** method, the text displayed can be made dependent on information gleaned from the visitor. This can include "external" information, such as the visitor's browser type and version, the date and time, and the number of pages previously visited. It can also include information provided by the visitor by means of prompt boxes.

TAGS OR AN EVENT HANDLER

If you want to write anything to the browser window that includes any of this information, you must use the **document. write** method; and, since it is a JavaScript command, this has to appear either between <script> and </script> tags, or within an event handler.

DOCUMENT.WRITE SYNTAX

To use the **document. write()** method, the information that you want to write to the screen must be placed within quotation marks between parentheses after the command, leaving no letter spaces except those within the text string: **document.write("Add your text here")**.

THE DOCUMENT. WRITE COMMAND

● Here is a simple example of JavaScript code that uses the **document. write**() command. All it does is write the opening four lines of one of Shakespeare's sonnets to the browser window; though not, in this case, in response to external information.

```
Writing with Javascript - Notepad
File  Edit  Search  Help
<HTML>
<HEAD>
<TITLE>Writing with Javascript</TITLE>
</HEAD>
<BODY>

<H4>Lines from Shakespeare's Sonnet XVIII</H4>

<SCRIPT language=javascript>
document.write("Shall I compare thee to a summer's day?");
document.write("Thou art more lovely and more temperate");
document.write("Rough winds do shake the darling buds of May");
document.write("And summer's lease hath all too short a date:");
</SCRIPT>
```

● Note that the lines are displayed in the browser window as one continuous line of text. No space is left between the end of one line and the beginning of the next.

```
Writing with Javascript - Microsoft Internet Explorer
File  Edit  View  Favorites  Tools  Help
Back   Forward   Stop  Refresh  Home   Search  Favorites  Histo
Address  C:\my javascript folder\Writing with Javascript.htm
```

Lines from Shakespeare's Sonnet XVIII

Shall I compare thee to a summer's day?Thou art more lovely and m
winds do shake the darling buds of MayAnd summer's lease hath all t

● If you intend the text to be displayed in one single line, it is necessary to leave a space at the end of a line. If you want the text to appear on several lines, add line breaks at the end of each line by using the **
** tag, as we see in this example.

```
2 - Notepad

h Javascript</TITLE>


kespeare's Sonnet XVIII</H4>

avascript>
all I compare thee to a summer's day?<br>");
ou art more lovely and more temperate<br>");
ugh winds do shake the darling buds of May<br>");
d summer's lease hath all too short a date:");
```

● The HTML line breaks divide the verse into separate lines. You can format text using HTML commands within the quotation marks of the **document.write** command.

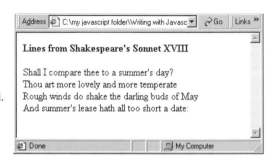

CONCATENATION

Concatenating is the joining together of elements into a series and is a process that is often carried out in programming. You can concatenate several text strings in the same line of a **document.write** command by using the "plus" sign. In an earlier

example , we saw how to detect a visitor's browser type and then write to the web page. This is an example of writing dynamically to the page. The output of the page is dependent on the identification of the browser.

● Breaking this code down, the line to be written is in three parts:
1 "**I see you're using the**" and the opening of the bold text tag.
2 +**navigator.appName**+. This identifies the application name (the **appName** property) of the navigator object and displays the output in bold.
3 The third part closes the bold tag and displays the word **browser** and a period to end the line.

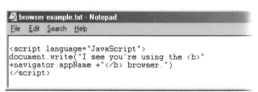

Identifying the web browser

USING COMMENTS IN JAVASCRIPT

We saw in the last chapter ⌐ how to use comments in HTML to hide the JavaScript from older browsers. "Comments" also have a second use and a second meaning when compiling, because they can also be used within the JavaScript in order to write notes to yourself that will not be seen on the web page. Such comments are preceded or contained within comment tags, and the tags used will depend on whether you want to "comment out" a single line or several lines of notes. When writing a page containing JavaScript code, these comments can be a considerable aid in writing your code, allowing you to leave reminders for when you return to writing.

JAVASCRIPT COMMENTS

● JavaScript comments enable you to intersperse your lines of code with lines of "invisible" explanatory text. Some of your comments will be temporary editing-in-progress notes, but you may choose to leave others in the code to remind you what you were thinking of at the time of writing when you return to remove or improve the code.

● If correctly formatted, your comments will not be displayed by the web browser, so anything can be typed following a comment tag.

```
comments - Notepad
File   Edit   Search   Help
<html>
<head>
<title>Javascript comments</title>
</head>

<script language="JavaScript">

document.write("Single line comments,<br>")
//Use this for single line comments

document.write("and multi-line comments,<br>")
/* Use these symbols for comments that run
 * over several lines. This is a lot tidier
 * and makes it much easier to pick out in a
 * page of code.
*/

document.write("and comments at the end of lines<br>") /

document.write("are <b>all</b> invisible in the browser

</script>

</html>
```

COVER YOUR TRACKS

Comments are not invisible to anyone who can read your source code, and any reader can do this simply by choosing **Source** from Internet Explorer's **View** menu or by opening the HTML document in a text reader. Therefore, you may wish to remove some of your comments before making your web pages available on the web.

POP-UP BOXES

One of the easiest ways to enliven your web pages and directly involve any visitors to your site is to use JavaScript's Alert, Confirm, and Prompt pop-up dialog boxes.

JAVASCRIPT DIALOG BOXES

The three kinds of JavaScript dialog boxes share one important characteristic. Once any one of them has popped up on-screen, all activity within the web page is frozen until an appropriate button in the dialog box is clicked. For example, once an Alert box has popped up, everything freezes until the **OK** button has been clicked. On-screen Alert boxes cannot be sent to the back of the browser window. Nor can you click within the main part of the browser window when an Alert box is displayed. The only possible action is to click the **OK** button in the box. This same suspension of activity holds true for the Confirm and Prompt boxes.

THE JAVASCRIPT POP-UP BOXES

● The Alert box ▯ is the simplest kind of box, and it is used mainly to capture the attention of the visitor.

● The Confirm box ▯ is also used in this way, but has a **Cancel** button so that the visitor also has the choice of refusing an option.

● The Prompt box ▯ takes the process one stage further by prompting the visitor to input information of some kind.

 27 Alert Boxes

28 Prompt Boxes

 30 Confirm Boxes

THE CASE IN QUESTION

If you have wondered why capital letters are found throughout the variables, functions, and other names used in JavaScript, the simple answer is convention. It doesn't matter whether you use the spelling **myvariable**, **MyVariable**, or **myVARIABLE**, but the way in which you spell it in the main body of the document should then match the case exactly, or your code may fail. For that reason, most people tend to use lower-case for functions and variables, reserving upper-case for the initial letter of subsequent words within the name, for example, **myVariable.**

ALERT BOXES

The alert method is used mainly to catch the visitor's attention. For example, one line of JavaScript can create a simple welcome announcement. An Alert box can also announce the results of more complicated JavaScript detection scripts, such as detecting whether the visitor has all the plug-ins necessary to view your site. You can choose to make any complex announcement that you like, but the code for launching the Alert box is very straightforward, as this example shows.

A WELCOMING ALERT BOX

● This example shows how to produce an Alert box that welcomes visitors to the "WebVerse" site. Whatever the content, the syntax works just the same.

● The status bar shows that the appearance of the Alert box has frozen the loading of the web page. As the **window.alert** code is in the head, the page will not load further until the **OK** button has been clicked.

```
alert.htm - Notepad
File  Edit  Search  Help
<html>
<title>WebVerse</title>
<script language="JavaScript">
window.alert("Welcome to WebVerse: the finest English
poetry on the Web. Press OK to continue.");
</script>
<body>
<h4>Welcome to WebVerse: a collection of the finest English
```

Microsoft Internet Explorer

⚠ Welcome to WebVerse: the finest English poetry on the Web. Press OK to continue.

OK

Opening page file://C:\my javascript   My Computer

PROMPT BOXES

The JavaScript Prompt box provides a text field in which the visitor to your web page can type an answer in response to a question. The box has an **OK** button, a **Cancel** button, and a text box to hold the response typed by the visitor. The Prompt box must be closed by clicking one of the buttons before being able to continue. The Prompt box enables you to capture the data typed there and use it elsewhere. How this information is subsequently used depends on the requirements of the web page and the skill and inventiveness of the author.

THE PROMPT BOX IN ACTION

● In this typical example, the visitor is invited to type his or her name into a field on the Prompt box and click the **OK** button.

● The visitor's name then appears in an on-screen greeting, which remains until the **OK** button is clicked.

● The web page that then appears in the browser window incorporates the visitor's name within the text. The JavaScript code that makes all this happen can be seen on the opposite page.

A collection of the finest English poetry

Welcome to WebVerse Josh.

This is an online guide to English poetry, providing links to some of the many collections of online verse, literary magazines, poetry discussion sites and so on.

This site mainly exists as an additional resource for a weekly e-mail newsletter compiled by a group of enthusiasts here in London. You'll find plenty to interest you on this site, but you'll find much more information if you subscribe to our newsletter.

USING VARIABLES WITH PROMPT BOXES

● As this code shows, in order to use what your visitor has typed, you need to create a variable name. The **window.prompt()** code captures the visitor's first name for you, but you can only use it if you associate that input with a variable name (e.g. **vName**).

● The variable can then be placed anywhere on the web page when used in conjunction with the **document.write()** command ⌐.

```
webverse.htm - Notepad
File  Edit  Search  Help

<html>
<title>WebVerse</title>
<script language="JavaScript">
var vName=prompt("What's your name?","");
alert("Hi " +vName+ " !");
</script>

<body>
<p><img src="images/wv.png" width="128" height="51"></p>
<p><b>A collection of the finest English poetry </b></p>
<p>
<script language="JavaScript">
document.write("Welcome to WebVerse " +vName+ ".")
</script>
<p>This is an online guide to English poetry, providing links
to some of the many collections of online verse, literary
magazines, poetry discussion sites and so on.
<p> This site mainly exists as an additional resource for a
weekly e-mail newsletter compiled by a group of enthusiasts
here in London. You'll find plenty to interest you on this
site, but you'll find much more information if you subscribe
to our newsletter.
<p> <a href="subs.htm">Subscribe</a>
<br>

</html>
```

Place the variable anywhere on the page ●

WINDOW.PROMPT SYNTAX

The prompt method must be used within <**script**> tags. The first string comprises the contents of the pop-up dialog box (usually the question that you are asking the visitor). In the code, you define the question exactly as you would for an Alert box. With the **window. prompt()** method, however, you can use an optional second text string to determine the text that will appear in the text field. This is usually filled with something helpful for the

visitor like "Type your reply here," and the visitor can immediately overtype it. If the second string is kept blank (i.e. you just use the quotation marks with nothing between them) and the visitor clicks **OK** without typing anything in the text box, nothing will appear in the appropriate position on the web page. To create a variable in

JavaScript, first choose a name for the variable, and then state what that variable name represents, using the following syntax: **var yourVariableName =value**. You can pick any name you choose for a variable, but it is more helpful to give it a descriptive name that shows what it contains.

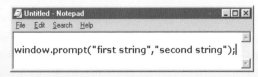

```
Untitled - Notepad
File  Edit  Search  Help

window.prompt("first string","second string");
```

CONFIRM BOXES

Confirm boxes are essentially Alert boxes that offer a choice of two response buttons: **OK** or **Cancel** (which is the same as Yes or No). There is very little point in using the **window.confirm**() method unless you can do something useful with the response typed by the visitor. To make the most of this **OK** or **Cancel** response, you need to learn how to use the **if...else** statement in JavaScript.

USING JUST THE IF... STATEMENT

● Here is a simple example that shows you can sometimes get the result you want merely by using the **if** clause. Clicking on the **subscribe** link brings up a Confirm box.

● The code that controls the Confirm box provides a conditional clause. This determines the effect of clicking on the **OK** button.

```
<html>
<head>
<script language="JavaScript">

if (confirm("To subscribe to the newsletter
click OK."))
{
location.href='subscribe.htm'
}

</script>

</head>
</html>
```

● If the visitor clicks the **OK** button, he or she will be taken to the URL defined in the line beginning **location.href**.

● The visitor is now taken to the defined URL (in this case, the subscription page **subscribe.htm**).

● However, if the visitor clicks the **Cancel** button, he/she will remain on the same page, since no other action has been defined.

● To provide a second option, you need to use the **else** statement.

● In this example, the **else** statement is used to define a second URL (in this case, **nonsubs.htm**), to which the visitor will be sent if he or she clicks the **Cancel** button.

```
<html>
<head>
<script language="JavaScript">

if (confirm("To subscribe to the newsletter
click OK."))
{
location.href='subscribe.htm'
}

else
{
location.href='nonsubs.htm'
}

</script>
```

● Now that the **else** clause has been written into the JavaScript, clicking the **Cancel** button will do more than leave the visitor in the original window.

● Instead, the window **nonsubs.htm** opens, as defined in the **else** clause. This window is being used to offer the visitor, who has opted not to subscribe to the newsletter, further choices within the website.

WINDOW.CONFIRM SYNTAX

The **window.confirm()** statement produces a pop-up window that offers the visitor a choice of actions. He or she can choose to accept a course of action by clicking the **OK** button, or reject it by clicking the **Cancel** button. The choice presented to the visitor is composed of the text you have typed between the brackets within quotation marks. Clicking **OK** takes the visitor to the location defined in the code. The use of the **else...** clause can be used to direct the visitor to an alternative page (rather than back to the original) if he or she clicks **Cancel**.

SOME JAVASCRIPT TERMINOLOGY

If you want to take your web page authoring skills beyond simple coding and communicate with other authors, you will need to understand the "hierarchy" on which JavaScript is built; this includes understanding the relationships of the three principal concepts of "object," "property," and "method." These examples show only a few of the properties and methods relating to the window object, but the principles apply to all JavaScript objects, properties, and methods.

OBJECT

● An object in JavaScript is an entity that can usually be broken down into sub-categories or parts. It can also have things done to it, or be acted upon. Objects include **window**, **form**, **image**, and **button**.

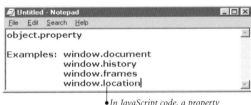

● In grammatical terms, an object is the JavaScript equivalent of a noun

PROPERTY

● A property in JavaScript is a quality that helps define an object – by providing a subcategory, or by describing a noun. The properties of an image, for example, are its **name**, **border**, **height**, and **width**.

● In JavaScript code, a property immediately follows the object it defines, separated by a period

METHOD

● A method describes an action that can be applied to an object. In this chapter, the **alert**, **confirm**, and **prompt** methods of the window object are described.

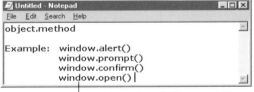

● In JavaScript, the method acts on an object in the way that a verb acts on a noun

MOUSEOVERS

Mouseover describes certain activities within the browser window that occur as a direct result of the movement of the mouse cursor or the clicking of the mouse button.

FUNCTIONS OF THE STATUS BAR

The text that appears in the web browser's status bar can provide useful information when you are viewing web pages. The changes in the contents of the status bar are often triggered by the movement and action of the mouse cursor.

THE STATUS BAR

● The status bar is at the bottom of the web browser window. Text in the status bar can change according to an activity currently taking place or that has just taken place in the browser window.

● For example, the text in the status bar will tell you that a web page is opening and will give you the URL of that site, as this example demonstrates.

● *The status bar shows the URL of the document being loaded*

● The status bar also tells you when a document has loaded by displaying the word **Done**.

● *Done appears when the document has been loaded*

MAKING MORE OF THE STATUS BAR · 35

● It also reveals the URL of a link when the mouse is moved over the hyperlink text or image, but as we will see below, the URL may not always be the most useful piece of information. This is where JavaScript can help.

MAKING MORE OF THE STATUS BAR

By using JavaScript to define the **window.status** property, you can use the status bar to provide useful information when the mouse cursor is held over a hyperlink. This can make your web pages more interesting and dynamic.

USING ONMOUSEOVER
● In the example shown here, the URL contained in this hyperlink (as it appears between the <**a href**> and </**a**> tags of the HTML code for the web page) will appear in the status bar by default when the mouse cursor is held over the hyperlinked text.

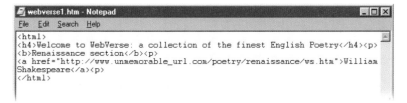

● Although the URL is fictional, its length is typical of many web pages, and because of its length only part of it is visible in the status bar.

● This information, which will not even fit in the status bar, does very little. However, it is possible to use **window.status** to make useful and interesting text appear in the status bar when the mouse is over the hyperlink.

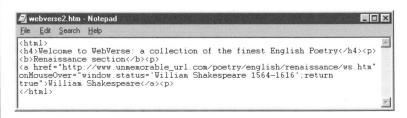

```
webverse2.htm - Notepad
File  Edit  Search  Help
<html>
<h4>Welcome to WebVerse: a collection of the finest English Poetry</h4><p>
<b>Renaissance section</b><p>
<a href="http://www.unmemorable_url.com/poetry/english/renaissance/ws.htm"
onMouseOver="window.status='William Shakespeare 1564-1616';return
true">William Shakespeare</a><p>
</html>
```

● The **onMouseOver** code in this example causes the text "**William Shakespeare 1564-1616**" to appear in the status bar when the mouse moves over the **William Shakespeare** hyperlink.

● However, the new status bar text remains even after the mouse is moved away from the hyperlink. This can be changed by using **onMouseOut**.

ONMOUSEOVER SYNTAX

This code will cause the text within single quotes to appear in the status bar when the mouse moves over the hyperlink. It will remain there until the page is reloaded or the mouse moves over another hyperlink. The onMouseOut event handler can be used to remove this status bar text 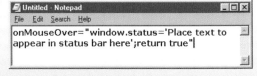.

```
Untitled - Notepad
File  Edit  Search  Help
onMouseOver="window.status='Place text to
appear in status bar here';return true"
```

37 Using **onMouseOut**

USING ONMOUSEOUT

● This code (line 6 in the code shown below) causes the text string within the single quote marks (i.e., nothing) to appear in the status bar when the mouse is moved off the hyperlink.

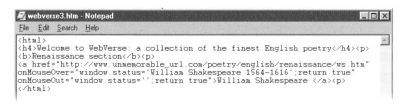

```
<html>
<h4>Welcome to WebVerse: a collection of the finest English poetry</h4><p>
<b>Renaissance section</b><p>
<a href="http://www.unmemorable_url.com/poetry/english/renaissance/ws.htm"
onMouseOver="window.status='William Shakespeare 1564-1616';return true"
onMouseOut="window.status='';return true">William Shakespeare </a><p>
</html>
```

● When the mouse is moved over the hyperlink the text defined in the **onMouseOver** code appears in the status bar, as it did before.

● Now, however, when the mouse is moved off the hyperlink, the text in the status bar disappears. If a text string had been placed between the single quotation marks, this would now appear in the status bar.

The text is removed from the status bar

ONMOUSEOUT SYNTAX

When used in conjunction with the **onMouseOver** code, the **onMouseOut** code will cause the text within single quotes to appear in the status bar when the mouse moves over the hyperlink. Because nothing appears between the single quotes in the example on this page, the text disappears and nothing appears in its place.

```
onMouseOut="window.status='';return true"
```

DOING IT WITH PICTURES

The most widely used kind of mouseover involves image swapping. The examples over the next few pages feature an effect known as a mouse rollover, a very commonly used technique that can be applied to any kind of image swapping.

1 NAMING YOUR ARTWORK

● The example here uses the very common effect of a button being depressed and released. Creating this effect is simple.

● We are using just two images, and, to keep things simple, they are called **off.jpg** and **on.jpg**, to reflect the placing of the cursor.

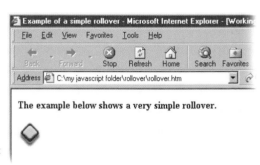

2 WRITE THE HTML CODE

● Create a link to the image that will appear when the page is loaded. This will be the only image visible on older browsers that are unable to display JavaScript rollovers. The image is called **off.jpg**. The `<img>` details need to be placed between the `<a href>` and `</a>` tags.

● There are three elements to the image tag. These are **Src**, **border**, and **name**.

● **Src.** States the image's location. After typing the code, place the image name between double quotes and include a path name if the image is in a folder other than the HTML document.

● The **border**. Setting the border at **0** removes the default border around images.

● The **name** tag. In this example, the image space has been named "image" ◻.

```
<html>
<title>Example of a simple rollover</title>
<body>
<h4>The example below shows a very simple rollover. </h4>

<img src="off.jpg" border=no name="image"></a>

</body>
</html>
```

◿
40 The
    name tag

3 WRITING THE JAVASCRIPT

● Now it is time to insert the code for the rollover.

● The code loads the image file **on.jpg** when the mouse cursor moves over the existing image (**off.jpg**), replacing the initial button image and creating the illusion that the button has been pushed in.

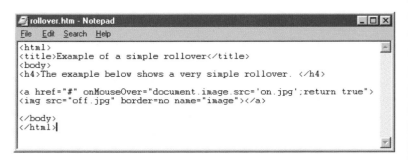

```
rollover.htm - Notepad                                    _ □ ×
File  Edit  Search  Help
<html>
<title>Example of a simple rollover</title>
<body>
<h4>The example below shows a very simple rollover. </h4>

<a href="#" onMouseOver="document.image.src='on.jpg';return true">
<img src="off.jpg" border=no name="image"></a>

</body>
</html>
```

● Until an **onMouseOut** command has been added, the button will stay pushed in even when the mouse cursor is moved away. The image space will continue to be occupied by **on.jpg**.

The example below shows

The example below shows

4 ADDING ONMOUSEOUT

● To complete the rollover and return off.jpg to the image space you need to add the **onMouseOut** command. Its position immediately follows the **onMouseOver** statement, but it still remains between the <**a href**> and <**/a**> HTML tags.

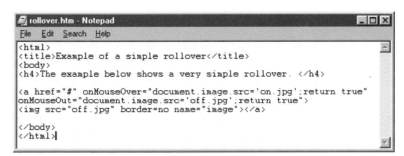

```
rollover.htm - Notepad                                    _ □ ×
File  Edit  Search  Help
<html>
<title>Example of a simple rollover</title>
<body>
<h4>The example below shows a very simple rollover. </h4>

<a href="#" onMouseOver="document.image.src='on.jpg';return true"
onMouseOut="document.image.src='off.jpg';return true">
<img src="off.jpg" border=no name="image"></a>

</body>
</html>
```

MAKING THE IMAGE A LIVE HYPERLINK

● To keep things simple, in this example we have used a dead link (#) for the image. If anyone clicks on the image, nothing will happen. Placing a live link here is simply a matter of replacing # with the appropriate URL.

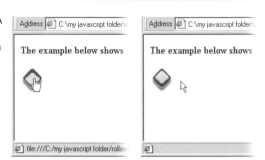

The name tag

It helps to think of the area on the page identified by the **name** tag as the space that the image occupies. The files **on.jpg** and **off.jpg** will occupy the space called **image**, depending on the cursor's action.

PRELOADING IMAGES

You can use JavaScript to preload images. This means that while your web page is first loading in the visitor's browser window, you can send the specified images to the browser cache, a folder on your computer that stores recently accessed web pages. If a web page is cached here, the browser can access it much more quickly than from a remote server. Certain images required for rollovers are not visible when the page has loaded. These are the images that can be usefully preloaded into the cache, so that they really spring into life when needed rather than being subject to the slight delay that usually happens while they are being downloaded from the web.

PRELOADING ON.JPG

● The code to make **on.jpg** appear, when we rollover **off.jpg**, goes into the body of the web page, but the code for preloading **on.jpg** goes into the `<head>` tags within script tags.

```
<head>
<script language="JavaScript">
Image1=new Image(20,20)
Image1.src="on.jpg"
</script>
</head>
```

PRELOADING MULTIPLE IMAGES

Image1 is a variable and you can choose any name you like for this, but it is always advisable to keep things simple. The information in brackets after **new Image** tells the browser the size of the image in pixels. It is saying "Reserve me a space with these dimensions on the page and fill it with the new image called Image1. I am just about to tell you where you can find Image1." **Image1.src** provides that location. If you want to preload more than one image, simply repeat the formula, keeping everything within the script tags. For example:

Image2=new Image(100,50)
Image2.src="services2.jpg"
Image3=new Image(120,50)
Image3.src="contact2.jpg"

This tells the browser to preload two more images with the dimensions in pixels and gives them both variable names (**Image2** and **Image3**). Initially, this profusion of names for what seem to be the same images can seem confusing, but, once grasped, it is really very simple.

HOW IT WORKS

In this example, **Image1** ❶ is the name that identifies the space into which the image **off.jpg** ❷ is loaded. This space is filled when the web page is first displayed. If the visitor doesn't move the mouse cursor over that space (i.e. that image), then nothing will happen. If the mouse cursor is moved over the space named **Image1**, however, the browser first checks the cache folder to see if any images have been preloaded for use in that space, it will find **on.jpg** ❸, which is the image that the browser is calling for.

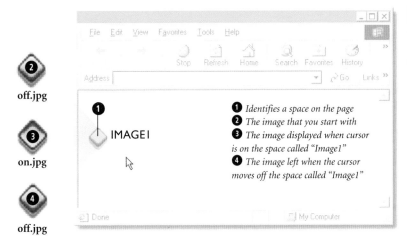

off.jpg ❷

on.jpg ❸

off.jpg ❹

❶ Identifies a space on the page
❷ The image that you start with
❸ The image displayed when cursor is on the space called "Image1"
❹ The image left when the cursor moves off the space called "Image1"

NEW WINDOWS

Have you ever wondered how some websites use pop-up windows to enhance their content? These sites are probably using JavaScript's **window.open**() and **window.close**() commands.

THE WINDOW OPEN() METHOD

The **open**() method of the window object creates new windows when a link or button is clicked while keeping the original window open. In addition to specifying the contents of a new window, you can also determine its dimensions and use of features such as toolbar and scrollbar. Some web page links lead to a pop-up text box rather than another web page, but the text box is probably a new web page. JavaScript has been used to strip the new web page of its features, which can be deactivated as easily as typing "**feature=no**" in a line of JavaScript.

WINDOW.OPEN SYNTAX

"URL"
If the HTML document is in the same folder (directory) as the main page, just type its name (e.g., **pagetoload.htm**). If it is in another directory, type the path (e.g., **anotherfolder/pagetoload .htm**). If the document is on another server (and if you have the owner's permission to use it), type the full web address (e.g., **http://www.anotherserver .com/pagetoload.htm**).

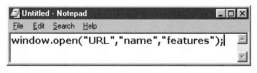

```
window.open("URL","name","features");
```

"NAME"
This name, surprisingly, does not appear in the title bar of the new web page. It is required for more advanced JavaScript effects, but in the example shown here it will have no effect on the appearance of the new window.

"FEATURES"
This contains all the optional features that determine the size and composition of the new window. If this third part of the string is left blank, the default window is opened with all the features in place .

OPENING A NEW WINDOW

● Opening a new window using JavaScript is simple. Just drop the lines of code: <**script language**="JavaScript"> **window. open("");</script>** into your HTML document. Of course, just opening a new window is only part of the process. If you dropped this code into one of your web pages, you would only display an empty box – or rather a window containing a pop-up error message. This is because you have not yet defined two important windows' parameters:
(1) The content you want to load into the new window;
(2) The event that will trigger the appearance of the new window and the loading of the content.

● The appearance of the new window is determined by the features that you decide it is to have. On the following pages, we will consider first how to define the new window's features, then how and when to load material into it.

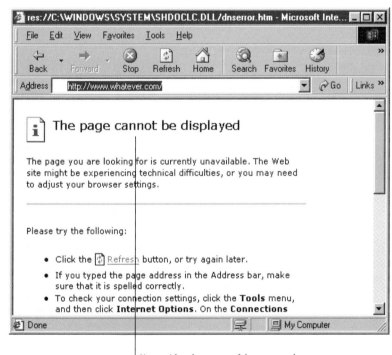

Since neither the content of the page nor the event that will trigger its appearance has been defined, the page displays an error message

DESIGNING THE NEW WINDOW

The appearance of web browsers can vary considerably, according to user preference. You need to cater to all browser setups when deciding which features to include or omit from any new windows you intend to create. Just because you can't see a particular browser feature on-screen, it doesn't mean that visitors to your website will have their browsers configured in the same way. So even if you have the toolbar switched off in your browser, remember to use the "**toolbar=no**" code if you want to ensure that it is absent from the new window when viewed in all browsers.

OPTIONAL CHOICES
This typical web page shows the features of the browser window that can be included or excluded when you use JavaScript to open a new window.

DEACTIVATING FEATURES
All these features are active by default when a new window is loaded. To deactivate any of them, use this code:

menubar=no	toolbar=no
location=no	scrollbars=no
status=no	resizeable=no

COMBINED NOTATIONS
Features can be set by using 1 (for "yes") and 0 (for "no"). Either notation works and they can also be combined.

KEY TO WINDOW FEATURES

❶ Menu bar
❷ Toolbar (back, forward buttons, etc.)
❸ Address bar (URL location field)
❹ Scrollbar
❺ Status bar
❻ Resize corner

DEFINING OTHER FEATURES

There are various other optional features that can be incorporated into a new window, but some of these are "JavaScript 1.2-compliant" only, which means that they will not work in earlier versions of Internet Explorer, Netscape Navigator, and some other browsers.

The most useful of these features enables you to define the position on the screen where the new window will pop up. Both the x and y coordinates of the top left corner of the new window can be defined in terms of the number of pixels from the left and the top of your on-screen desktop. The syntax for doing this is:

screenx=pixels (for the x coordinate)
screeny=pixels (for the y coordinate).

The effect of typing in "**screenx=200**," for example, will be to position the top left corner of the new window 200 pixels from the left of your on-screen desktop.

DEFINING WIDTH AND HEIGHT

To define the dimensions of the new window, use the width and height settings.

width=pixels (e.g., **width=300**)
height=pixels (e.g., **height=320**)

Separate each feature setting with a comma: "**width=350,menubar=no,status= no,resizeable=no.**"

USING YES FOR FEATURES

When you are looking at other people's source code (which is highly recommended if you decide to learn more about JavaScript), you will notice the use of "**feature=yes.**" Why bother to deliberately activate a feature when all features are active by default? Using "**yes**" actually has a different effect on the new window's composition. If you use "**feature=yes**" you specifically activate that feature and deactivate all the others. It is the equivalent to saying, "All features should be deactivated apart from the ones I am expressly stating are active (by using "**feature= yes**")." Whichever method you use is purely a matter of personal preference.

Loading an Existing Document

Having decided on the composition of the new window, we can concentrate on the material that will go into it. There are two main methods for generating content for new windows. You can generate the content of a new web page from an existing web page, or from content loaded with the main web page and generated dynamically (or "on the fly"). Here we will look at the first of these methods.

DEFINING THE WEB PAGE TO BE INSERTED

● To fill this new window with another HTML document, replace the URL part of the syntax as required: **document. write("URL," "name," "features")** . You will need to have already created the document that you intend to load into the new window, unless you are going to use a web page that you have found on another site. (You must have asked for and received the site owner's permission before using a web page from another website in this way.) In the example shown here, the main page is called sonnet.htm and the document to be loaded into the page is called 18.htm. These are seen in action below.

TRIGGERING THE ACTION

● You have now decided on the features for your new window and the content that will be loaded into it. All that's left to decide now is what will trigger the appearance of the new window. A typical and straightforward solution is to use a hyperlink or a button. The example here (for the code, see opposite) uses a hyperlink and the **onClick** event handler to open the new window.

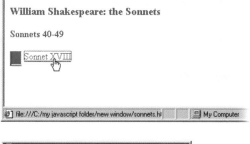

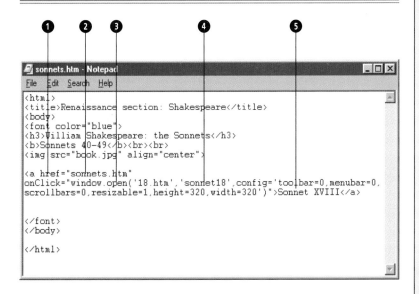

```
sonnets.htm - Notepad
File  Edit  Search  Help
<html>
<title>Renaissance  section: Shakespeare</title>
<body>
<font color="blue">
<h3>William Shakespeare: the Sonnets</h3>
<b>Sonnets 40-49</b><br><br>
<img src="book.jpg" align="center">

<a href="sonnets.htm"
onClick="window.open('18.htm','sonnet18',config='toolbar=0,menubar=0,
scrollbars=0,resizable=1,height=320,width=320')">Sonnet XVIII</a>


</font>
</body>

</html>
```

ELEMENTS OF THE CODE

❶ Because we are using the onClick event handler here, there is no need to use <script> tags. All the script is contained within the HTML anchor tags <a href> and </a>.

❷ First type the name of the document from which the new window will be "called" – in other words, the document in which you are typing this code, which in this case is sonnets.htm.

❸ Next comes the onClick="window. open()" command. Note the quotation marks enclosing the window.open() command, and the parentheses that will contain all the information pertaining to your new window. These are essential elements of the code.

❹ Place all the parameters relating to your new window (everything that this chapter has been dealing with so far) within the parentheses. This example shows the following information: The document to be loaded is called 18.htm. The window's name (for coding and not display purposes) is sonnet18. The features available in the new window are then defined. The new window will have no toolbar, menubar, scrollbars, and it will remain the same size. The height and width are defined as 320 pixels tall and 320 pixels wide.

❺ Finally, the text that will provide the visible hyperlink on the page is given – Sonnet XVIII.

WRITING "ON THE FLY" TO THE NEW WINDOW

The second main method of filling a new web page is to use information embedded in the HTML code of the main page. This information remains hidden until the visitor requests it (usually by clicking a link), and it is loaded into the new window.

CODE BREAKDOWN

● The following code is placed between `<script>` tags within the document's `<head>` tags. To write to a new window, use the **document.write**() method ⬚. You need to create a function in this part of the code and then call this function within the `<body>` section.

KEY TO CODE ELEMENTS

❶ *First create a function. In this case, it is called* **rhymenote.** *The function comprises everything between the curly brackets.*

❷ *This creates a variable called* **rhymewin.** *Again, the name is entirely up to you.*

❸ =**window.open("……")**
All the parameters relating to the new window are placed within these parentheses.

❹ **document.write** *This instructs the browser to use the* **document.write** *method to write everything within the parentheses in the new window. Here it comprises an entire web page, enclosed between the* `<html>` *and* `</html>` *tags.*

❺ **sonnet.htm** *First type the name of the document from which the new window will be "called" – in other words, the document in which you are typing this code.*

❻ **onClick** *Since we are using the* **onClick** *event handler here, there is no need to use* `<script>` *tags. The script is contained within the HTML anchor tags* `<a href>` *and* `</a>`.

```
File  Edit  Search  Help
<html>
<title>Renaissance section: Shakespe
<head>
<script language="JavaScript">
function rhymenote()
{
   var rhymewin=window.open("","rhym
   rhymewin.document.write("<html><h
   14 lines. The <i>Shakespearean</i
   usually closing in a rhyming couple
   epigrammatic quality." +"</html>");
}
</script>
</head>

<body>
<font color="blue"><h3>William Shake
<b>Sonnets 11-20</b><br><br>
<img src="book.jpg" align="center">
<a href="sonnets.htm"
onClick="window.open('16.htm','<b
resizable=1,height=320,width=320')">

<img src="book.jpg" align="center">
<a href="sonnets.htm"
onClick="window.open('17.htm','sonne
resizable=1,height=320,width=320')">

<img src="book.jpg" align="center">
<a href="sonnets.htm"
onClick="window.open('18.htm','sonne
resizable=1,height=320,width=320')">

<h5>Notes on the <a href="sonnets.ht
scheme</a>.</h5>

</body>
</html>
```

USING THE FUNCTION

● As we have seen , a function (**rhymenote**) has been placed in the <**head**> part of the document. This is activated by clicking on the hyperlink

sonnet rhyme scheme .
● All the code in stage 4 within the HTML anchor tags <a href> and </a> is then written into the new window, causing the new web page to appear.

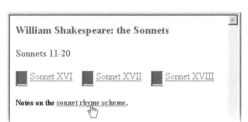

```
tle>


tus=yes,height=220,width=220");


t rhyme schemes</h3>" +"<p>Sonnets have
ty are written in iambic pentameter,
concluding couplet often has an



   the Sonnets</h3>


nfig='toolbar=0,menubar=0,scrollbars=0,
XVI</a>   


nfig='toolbar=0,menubar=0,scrollbars=0,
XVII</a>   


nfig='toolbar=0,menubar=0,scrollbars=0,
XVIII</a><br><br></font>


ick="rhymenote()">sonnet rhyme
```

6 **7** **8**

KEY TO CODE ELEMENTS

7 **"rhymenote()"** *This calls the function that was defined earlier* .
8 **sonnet rhyme scheme** *This is the text that appears on the web page as a hyperlink. Clicking this will cause the* **rhymenote** *function to work. In other words, the web page defined in* **4** *will be written into the new window defined in* **2** *and* **3**.

1 rhymenote

CLOSING A SECONDARY WINDOW

One of the main uses of a window without a menubar is as an "info box" – a pop-up window providing material that is meant to be read and closed. While the visitor can close the window by clicking the close [x] box in the top right of this mini-window, it is neater if you provide a "close" link or button as part of the page.

THE CLOSE COMMAND

● To trigger the **window.close** command, you will generally use the same technique that you employed to open it; i.e., a text hyperlink or a button.

● You then embed the close command into the material that is loaded into the new window. So, if you are loading a new document (e.g., **18.htm**), the **window.close** command must appear in the appropriate position on that page.

```
But thy eternal summer shall not fade,<br>
Nor lose possession of that fair thou ow'st,<br>
Nor shall death brag thou wander'st in his shade,<br>
When in eternal lines to time thou grow'st,<br>
So long as men can breathe, or eyes can see,<br>
So long lives this, and this gives life to thee.</font><br>
<br>

<a href="" onClick"self.close()">Close this window</a>

<html>
```

C:\my javascript folder\new

XVIII

Shall I compare thee to a summer
Thou art more lovely and more t
Rough winds do shake the darlir
And summer's lease hath all too
Sometime too hot the eye of hea
And often is his gold complexior
And every fair from fair sometim
By chance, or nature's changing
But thy eternal summer shall not
Nor lose possession of that fair t
Nor shall death brag thou wand∈
So long as men can breathe, or e
So long lives this, and this gives

Close this window

● *<a href= "" onClick= "self.close()">Close this window</a>*
Place this line of code within the HTML source code where you want it to appear on the web page (i.e. at the bottom of the page in the example)

THE "LINK METHOD"

To close a new window using a hyperlink, first create a link that goes nowhere! To do this, type the quotation marks but leave a blank where the linked document or URL would normally appear: <a href=""></a> Then type the text that will appear on the page as the hyperlink between the > < characters, as usual: <a href="">Close this window</a>. Then add the JavaScript code immediately after the blank quotation marks: <a href="" onClick= self.close( )">Close this window</a>.

HOW DOES THE LINK METHOD WORK?

When a visitor to this web page clicks the "Close this window" hyperlink, the browser attempts to go to the new page. Since there is no page to go to, the browser follows the instruction given by the JavaScript code and closes the page. (If you try typing a URL between the quote marks, you will see that the hyperlink will take you to that URL, overruling the JavaScript instruction).

USING A CLOSE BUTTON

● To use a "Close" button to close the new window, as this example shows, you need to place the JavaScript code in the position on the page where you intend for the button to appear. The obvious place in this example would seem to be the bottom of the page, so the code can be placed immediately before the closing </html> tag.

```
Nor lose possession of that fair thou ow'st,<br>
Nor shall death brag thou wander'st in his shade,<br>
When in eternal lines to time thou grow'st,<br>
So long as men can breathe, or eyes can see,<br>
So long lives this, and this gives life to thee.</font>
<br><br>

<form>
<input type="button" value="Close" onClick="self.close()">
</form>

<html>
```

And summer's lease hath a...
Sometime too hot the eye of
And often is his gold compl
And every fair from fair son
By chance, or nature's chan
But thy eternal summer shal
Nor lose possession of that
Nor shall death brag thou w
When in eternal lines to tim
So long as men can breathe
So long lives this, and this

onClick="self.close()." This part of the <form> code instructs the browser window to close when the button is clicked

HOW DOES THIS WORK?

When a visitor to this web page clicks the "Close" button, the page closes itself. To produce this page-closing button, create a button by using <form> and <input> tags. Whatever you choose for value, of course, will appear on the button itself, so keep it relatively brief. In this example, we have just used the word "Close."
<form>
<input type="button" value="Close">
</form>

The JavaScript event handler code is the same as that for closing a hyperlink. Place this immediately before the end of the input line.
<form>
<input type="button" value="Close" onClick=self.close( )>
</form>
When the close button is clicked, the page closes, and the visitor should now be returned seamlessly to the page from which he/she began.

GETTING HELP

**If your JavaScript code goes wrong, your browser will
sometimes (but not always) provide you with help in the form
of a JavaScript error message box.**

DEBUGGING THE JAVASCRIPT

If any of your JavaScript code contains errors, you will need to correct them before making the web page that contains them available to the public. This process is known as debugging. If you are lucky, it will involve only one or two typographical corrections. Sometimes – if, for example, there are major syntactical errors in the JavaScript – it might necessitate rebuilding your code line by line.

GETTING ADVICE FROM THE BROWSER
● If you have been working through the examples in the last chapter, typing the code into Notepad and testing it in your web browser as you go, you will almost certainly have seen one of these error message boxes, unless your typing skills are flawless!

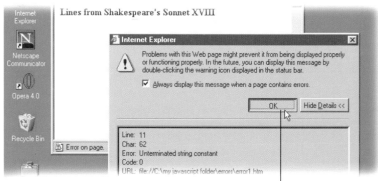

If there is a further error, the browser will inform you when you click OK.
Correcting the first error may stop all subsequent errors from occurring.

RECEIVING AN ERROR MESSAGE

Error message boxes can be very helpful, vague, or just confusing, depending on the kind of error detected and the type and version of the web browser that is being used to read the web page. The page may load, but the JavaScript fails to work. The only evidence that something is wrong may simply be a message in the status bar.

⚠ Done, but with errors on page.

Error messages can be vague

UNDERSTANDING THE DETAIL

When a JavaScript error message does appear in Internet Explorer, it usually contains the line and character position where the scripting problem has occurred. If you have been learning how to write your scripts using Notepad, or a similarly simple text editor, you will have little difficulty in finding where things have gone wrong. If you have copied-and-pasted a script from elsewhere (another web page or a script repository on the web, for example) or you have inserted a script created by a web design package (such as FrontPage or Dreamweaver), and need to rely on the information provided in the error message box, you will find that debugging can take considerably longer.

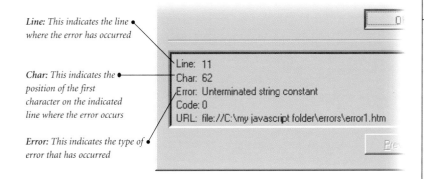

Line: *This indicates the line where the error has occurred*

Char: *This indicates the position of the first character on the indicated line where the error occurs*

Error: *This indicates the type of error that has occurred*

Line: 11
Char: 62
Error: Unterminated string constant
Code: 0
URL: file://C:\my javascript folder\errors\error1.htm

FIND AND FIX

● The error message in this example gives you enough information to locate the area causing all the problems.

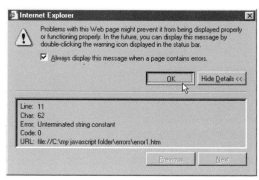

LOCATING THE ERROR

● Open the source code of the relevant HTML document in Notepad.

● Following the instructions in the error message, count down 11 lines from the top of the page, including blank lines.

● Now count 62 characters from the left of line 11.

● The error line in your JavaScript error message box can sometimes be a little cryptic, but, in this case, character 62 of line 11 leads us to the end of a string that fails to close a pair of double quotes (that

opened earlier on that line) after the line break <br> at the end of this line.

● Add the double quotes between the > and the), and you've fixed the problem that the error box has announced as an "unterminated string constant."

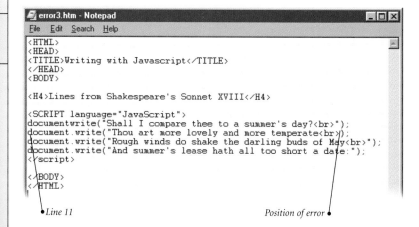

```
error3.htm - Notepad
File  Edit  Search  Help
<HTML>
<HEAD>
<TITLE>Writing with Javascript</TITLE>
</HEAD>
<BODY>

<H4>Lines from Shakespeare's Sonnet XVIII</H4>

<SCRIPT language="JavaScript">
documentwrite("Shall I compare thee to a summer's day?<br>");
document.write("Thou art more lovely and more temperate<br>);
document.write("Rough winds do shake the darling buds of May<br>");
document.write("And summer's lease hath all too short a date:");
</script>

</BODY>
</HTML>
```

● Line 11   Position of error ●

REPEAT THE PROCEDURE

● Now save the page and open the HTML document in your Web browser again. If the HTML document opens as you expected, with all the JavaScript code functioning correctly, you have solved the problem.

● If the browser then encounters another problem, you will need to address the new problem using the technique just described.

● Repeat the procedure as many times as necessary!

FINDING THE LINES

● If there is a marked discrepancy between your calculation of a line number and the number that appears in the browser's error message box, try turning off the Word Wrap feature in Notepad. You'll find it in the Edit menu.

● Some script editors and website design programs provide line numbers for you. When you view the source code, these may prove more helpful than Notepad when correcting errors in your scripts.

● In Macromedia's Dreamweaver, for example, you have the option of displaying line numbering alongside the HTML code. Simply click on the check box next to **Line Numbers** at the top of the page.

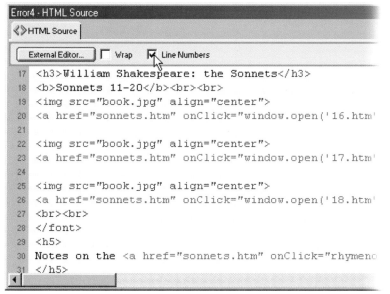

```
Error4 - HTML Source
<>HTML Source

  External Editor...    □ Wrap   ☑ Line Numbers

17  <h3>William Shakespeare: the Sonnets</h3>
18  <b>Sonnets 11-20</b><br><br>
19  <img src="book.jpg" align="center">
20  <a href="sonnets.htm" onClick="window.open('16.htm'
21
22  <img src="book.jpg" align="center">
23  <a href="sonnets.htm" onClick="window.open('17.htm'
24
25  <img src="book.jpg" align="center">
26  <a href="sonnets.htm" onClick="window.open('18.htm'
27  <br><br>
28  </font>
29  <h5>
30  Notes on the <a href="sonnets.htm" onClick="rhymeno
31  </h5>
```

*When you choose to view the source code in Macromedia's Dreamweaver, you can opt to view line numbers by checking the **Line Numbers** box at the top of the viewing area.*

ERROR WARNINGS IN INTERNET EXPLORER

If you are not seeing the kind of JavaScript error warning box described on these pages, perhaps this feature is inactive in your copy of Internet Explorer. If that is the case, turn it on right away. It may not be everything you need, but it can prove invaluable in sending you to the area of your script that is going wrong.

ACTIVATING ERROR NOTIFICATION

Choose **Internet Options** from the **Tools** menu of Internet Explorer.

Click the **Advanced** tab.
Place a check mark in the box next to **Display a notification about every script error**.

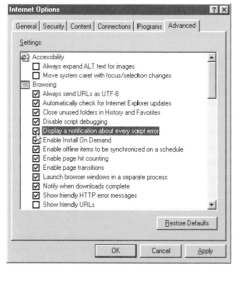

● Once you have carried
out these steps, click on the
OK button.

COMMON ERRORS IN JAVASCRIPT CODE

The two main types of error in JavaScript
are known as syntax errors and runtime
errors. This usually means that you have
either mistyped or omitted something.
Syntax errors often involve mistyped

quotation marks or parentheses. Runtime
errors are often caused by misspelled
commands. Both kinds of errors will cause
your web pages to behave erratically, or
they will stop loading in the browser.

A WORKING EXAMPLE

● Here we see source code
for a web page that uses a
simple level of interactivity.
The JavaScript code
consists of just a few lines:
a function within the
document's <**head**> tags
and an **onClick** event
handler within the
document's <**body**> tags.

```
File  Edit  Search  Help
<html>
<head>
<script language="JavaScript">

function whatYear()
{
var n=prompt("What year is it?");
confirm("Is it really now "+ n + " and we still
haven't returned to the moon?");
}

</script>
</head>

<body>
<form>
<input type="button" value="Answer me this..."
onClick="whatYear()">
```

● The web page invites the
user to click on the **Answer
me this** button.

● Clicking on the button causes a prompt box to appear, asking a question. The user keys the answer into the field below.

● The user's input is then output as part of the text that appears in an alert box that pops up.

● We will now introduce some deliberate errors and look at the resulting error messages provided by the web browser.

ROGUE PARENTHESES AND BRACKETS

● Opened parentheses and brackets that are not closed later on can be a major cause of script failure. This example shows a curly bracket in the last line that is closed but was never opened!

```
moon.htm - Notepad
File  Edit  Search  Help
<html>
<head>
<script language="JavaScript">

function whatYear()

var n=prompt("What year is it?");
confirm(Is it really now" + n + " and we still haven't
returned to the moon?");
}
```

● Netscape Navigator recognizes that there is an error and tells you how to find out more.

JavaScript error: Type 'javascript:' into Location for details

*To view JavaScript error messages in Netscape Navigator ●
(v4.75), follow the instructions in the browser's status bar*

● The error message explicitly states that the curly bracket has been omitted from its expected position before the body of the function, and the cursor line in the code shows where it should be.

```
Communicator Console - Netscape

JavaScript Error: file:/C|/MYJAVA~1/MOON.

missing { before function body.

var n=prompt("What year is it?");
      ^
```

●*The precise error is made clear for the user*

ROGUE QUOTATION MARKS

● Quotation marks also work in pairs. Confusion can be caused by apostrophes. Internet Explorer thinks the error here is the absence of a closing parenthesis, but in fact it is interpreting the apostrophe in **haven't** as a closing single quotation mark and so it expects a closing parenthesis after it.

● The best solution is to use double quotation marks if you are going to use any apostrophes, or you can sidestep the issue by avoiding contractions.

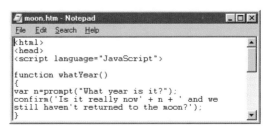

THE CASES IN QUESTION

● If you can't seem to detect that troublesome bug, make sure that all case-sensitive words match exactly, especially in functions and variables since these are words you have defined yourself. The problem here is very clearly stated by the Opera web browser. The function "whatYear" is defined, but the browser has never heard of the variable "whatyear," and it tells you so in its error message.

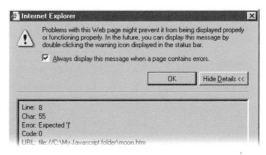

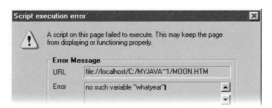

AUTOMATED SCRIPTING

**So far we have looked at using a simple text editor,
such as Notepad, to write JavaScript code as a script or directly
into an HTML document. There are alternatives…**

SOFTWARE: SCRIPT EDITORS

If you are likely to do much scripting, you may find it helpful to use software that works like a kind of enhanced text editor. Such programs take some of the routine keyboard work out of scripting, but still leave you in control of what you produce. You can find plenty of programs of this kind on software download sites such as Tucows at **www.tucows.com** or Winfiles at **www.winfiles.com**.

USING SCRIBBLER 2000
This example features a shareware program called Scribbler 2000 by Cream Software, which can be found at **www.creamsoft.com/scribbler**. The program produces code that is almost identical (and equally effective) to any coded-by-hand, Notepad-produced examples shown in this book so far. The example here shows how to use Scribbler 2000 to produce the kind of new window that was created in Chapter 6 .

A NEW WINDOW
IN SCRIBBLER 2000
● With the program installed and open on your PC, choose **Open new window** from the **Script** drop-down menu.

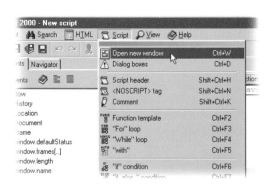

● In the **New window settings** dialog box, choose all the features you require the new window to have by defining the dimensions in the **Width** and **Height** boxes, and by placing a check mark in the appropriate **Settings** boxes.
● Finally, click on the OK button.

The OK button

● When you have defined the features of the new window, the program generates the JavaScript code in the two windows at right. The top window is for any code that you need to place within the <head> tags of the HTML document. The lower window is for code you need to place in the <body> tags of the same document.
● Click the **Copy to Clipboard** button to copy the relevant script to the clipboard for transfer into your HTML document.

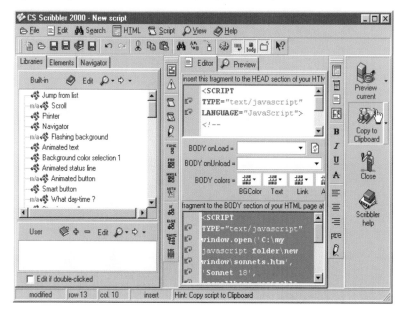

MICROSOFT'S FRONTPAGE EXPRESS

FrontPage Express is Microsoft's free web page editor that enables you to create and format web pages in an easy-to-use WYSIWYG (what you see is what you get) layout. It offers many of the features available in the full versions of FrontPage Editor and FrontPage Explorer, including the capability to insert JavaScript code.

ADDING YOUR OWN JAVASCRIPT CODE

● To add your own JavaScript code to an HTML document that you are creating using FrontPage Express, first choose **Script** from the **Insert** menu. The **Script** dialog box will appear.

● In the **Script** dialog box, click on the JavaScript radio button in the **Language** panel. Then type your code in the code box below and click on **OK**. There is no need to surround the code with <**script**> tags.

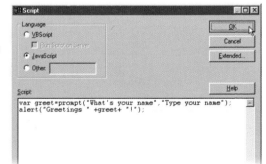

● The JavaScript code you have inserted into the HTML will now appear as a symbol on the page.

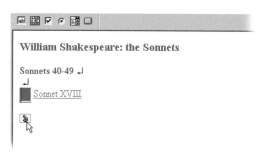

● To see the HTML source code, choose **HTML** from the **View** menu.

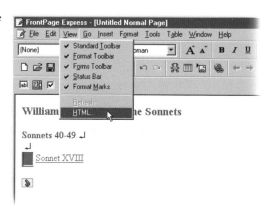

REVISING YOUR JAVASCRIPT

You can revise an existing script at any time when you are using Frontpage Express, simply by right-clicking the appropriate script icon in the Frontpage Express window and choosing **Script Properties** from the drop-down menu. This will open the **Script** window, revealing your Javascript code (in the Script window). Click **OK** when you have finished revising the script and then save the HTML document by

choosing **Save** from the **File** menu in the main Frontpage Express window.

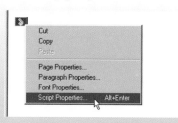

● In this example, FrontPage Express has been used to cause a User Prompt to appear, generated by the line of code beginning **var greet=prompt**. As this example shows, FrontPage Express has made very few modifications to the code

you typed in the code box, but it has carried out two important tasks. First, it has added comment tags to prevent it from being visible to non-JavaScript-enabled browsers ⌐]; and second, it has placed the necessary <script> tags around your code.

● If you opt to use such sophisticated web design packages as FrontPage Editor and Explorer to generate JavaScript code, you may find, when you look at the source code, that it turns out to be more complex than you were expecting.

The User Prompt is generated by the line of code beginning var greet=prompt

20 **Hiding JavaScript**

MACROMEDIA'S DREAMWEAVER

Macromedia's Dreamweaver is one of the best site-design packages available. Most of its JavaScript-related features (categorized as **Behaviors**), together with other advanced HTML effects, are accessed through the **Behaviors** window.

DREAMWEAVER'S BEHAVIOR MENUS

● In this example, we are going to use the **Open Browser Window** dialog box to set the features for a new pop-up window ⬚.

● Start by clicking the + button and choosing **Open Browser Window** from the drop-down menu.

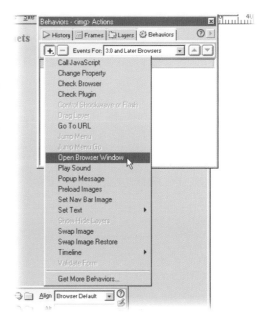

● Choose the features you require from the **Open Browser Window** dialog box and click on **OK**.

● Dreamweaver now automatically generates the JavaScript code and places it within the HTML source code for the page.

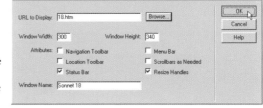

44 Designing the New Window

ADDING YOUR OWN SCRIPTS

● To place your own JavaScript within an HTML document that you are building using Dreamweaver, start by choosing **Script** from the **Insert** drop-down menu.

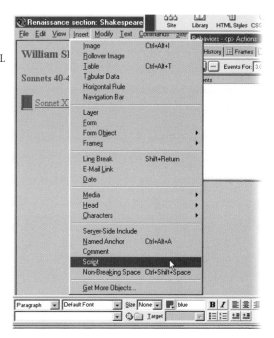

● In the **Insert Script** dialog box, choose **JavaScript** from the drop-down **Language** box.

● Type your script in the **Content** box. There is no need to key in **<script>** tags or comments within this box. Click on **OK**.

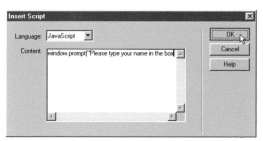

INSERTING A ROLLOVER IMAGE

● To insert a rollover image, start by choosing **Rollover Image** from the **Insert** drop-down menu.

● The **Insert Rollover Image** dialog box will open. Click the **Preload Rollover Image** check box if you want the rollover images to be preloaded ⌐.
● Then click on the first **Browse** button.

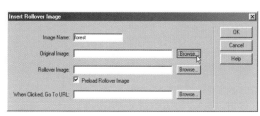

● In the **Original Image** dialog box, navigate to the image file you intend to use for the original image.
● Once it is selected, you will return to the **Insert Rollover Image** dialog box. Click on the second **Browse** button, navigate to the image file you intend to use for the rollover image, and click on **Select**.

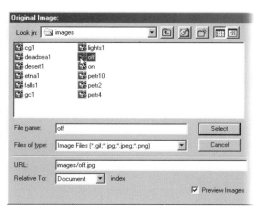

● Once the original and rollover images are named in the fields in the **Insert Rollover Image** dialog box, click on **OK**.

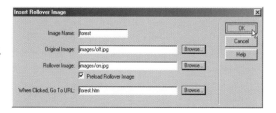

● The rollover will now be in place on your web page. This method reduces the need for you to know how to write code, but the code that it generates can be very confusing if you want to learn to do it for yourself.

SCRIPTS FROM THE WEB

The web can offer huge amounts of JavaScript code for all
levels of author. You will also find some excellent tutorials and
repositories of ready-made scripts.

READY-MADE SCRIPTS

One of the quickest ways to see the range
of JavaScript's capabilities is to visit one of
the many "script repositories" on the web,
which have scripts available for you to cut
and paste into your own documents.
Usually, you are asked to credit the author
in your HTML code or to place a shortcut
to the site on your web page. Many of
these sites give clear instructions about
how to copy and paste the script into your
own HTML document, and you can learn
a lot from the code.

WEBMONKEY
JAVASCRIPT LIBRARY

● HotWired's WebMonkey
is an essential site for any
web page author. The
Javascript code library
covers a wide range of
subjects and offers a large
number of free code
samples to use in your
source code. There is also a
wealth of information from
JavaScript authors that will
stimulate your own ideas
and help you write better
code. Or you can just copy
and paste the scripts,
marvel at the authors'
ingenuity, and leave the
learning for another day...

THE JAVASCRIPT SOURCE

● The JavaScript Source contains hundreds of free JavaScripts that you can copy and paste into your source code. Organized by category, each script is illustrated with a fully working example. You can also choose an option that enables you to have any JavaScript sent directly to your email address.

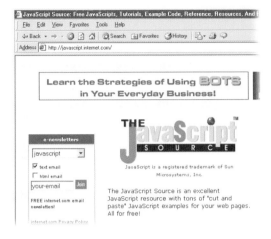

WEBSITE ABSTRACTION

● This site offers an excellent library of free JavaScript code as well as a broad range of JavaScript-related resources, including tutorials aimed at beginners to advanced-level users. The free JavaScripts are arranged in more than 20 top-level categories.

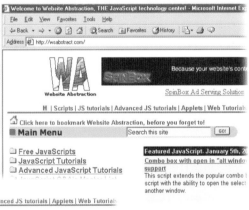

GLOSSARY

COMMENTS
Explanatory text that appears in source code but not on the page.

CONCATENATE
Run two or more strings together (using the character + between each) to create one longer string.

DOWNLOAD
The process of transferring a file from a remote computer to your computer.

EMBED
To place one block of code within another. JavaScript code is embedded within HTML.

EVENT HANDLERS
A JavaScript command (such as onClick or onSubmit) that is carried out when the user has executed the appropriate mouse or key movement.

EVENT
An action carried out by the user, such as moving or clicking the mouse, or entering or leaving a web page.

FREEWARE
Software that can be freely used and distributed but whose author retains copyright.

FUNCTION
A block of code containing a series of commands, identified by a single user-defined name.

GIF
Graphics Interchange Format. A compressed image format limited to 256 colors, suited to images with large areas of flat color, such as web graphics.

HOME PAGE
The main page of a website, usually called home.htm or index.htm, which is opened first when you visit a website.

HTML
Hypertext markup language. The "tagged" formatting language in which web pages are written.

HYPERLINK
Part of a web page (text, image, table, etc.) that links to a file or document on the internet.

HYPERTEXT
Text that links to other parts of a document, or to documents held on another computer.

ISP
Internet Service Provider. Any organization that provides access to the internet.

JPEG
Joint Photographic Experts Group. One of the most commonly used image formats on the internet, widely used for photographs.

LAYER
A container in Dreamweaver into which text, images, objects, and other layers can be loaded.

NETWORK
A group of interconnected computers that exchange data.

PATH
The address of a file on a computer system.

PIXEL
A unit of measurement for computer displays. A display consists of a series of pixels that display images on screen.

PNG
A widely used compressed image format on the web that, like the JPEG format, can display millions of colors.

ROLLOVER
In web pages, the swapping of one image for another when the mouse cursor passes over a specific image space, giving the effect of animation.

SERVER
Any computer that allows users to connect to it and share information and resources held on it. Also refers to the software that makes the information available for downloading.

SHAREWARE
Software that is made freely available for use on a try-before-you-buy basis.

STATUS BAR
The area along the bottom of the web browser window that shows a URL when the mouse cursor points to the hyperlink.

STRING
A value consisting of a series of alphanumeric characters enclosed in quotation marks.

UPLOAD
The process of transferring a file from your computer to a remote computer.

VARIABLE
A user-defined name that refers to a value. A variable can consist of a string.

INDEX

ACKNOWLEDGMENTS

PUBLISHER'S ACKNOWLEDGMENTS
Dorling Kindersley would like to thank the following:
Paul Mattock of APM, Brighton, for commissioned photography.
Microsoft Corporation for permission to reproduce screens
from within Microsoft® Windows® 98.
Cream Software, Website Abstraction.

Screen shots of Microsoft® Internet Explorer used
by permission from Microsoft Corporation.

Every effort has been made to trace the copyright holders.
The publisher apologizes for any unintentional omissions and would be pleased,
in such cases, to place an acknowledgment in future editions of this book.

All other images © Dorling Kindersley.
For further information see: www.dkimages.com

Microsoft® is a registered trademark of Microsoft Corporation
in the United States and/or other countries.